BUBS WITH THE NUBS

Audrey & Dawson
every good and perfect
thing comes from God.
Bethany Marshall

BY BETHANY MARSHALL
ILLUSTRATED BY SARAH VOGEL

THIS BOOK IS DEDICATED TO THE BOXER BREED
AND TO OUR VERY OWN BOUNCY BOXER, TIMBER,
ALSO KNOWN AS "BUBS WITH THE NUBS."

4

JUST ONE ENCOUNTER WITH A BOXER,
AND YOU'LL KNOW THESE THINGS ARE TRUE.

BOXERS ARE PLAYFUL, SMART, AND FRIENDLY.
SOME EVEN BELIEVE THEY'RE PART HUMAN TOO.

6

BOXERS ARE HUMOROUS
AND EXPRESSIVELY GOOFY.

WHEN HAPPY, YOU'LL SEE HOW
THEY LIKE TO SHAKE THEIR FURRY BOOTY.

THEIR LOVE LANGUAGE IS SIMPLE;
IT INVOLVES MAINLY TWO THINGS:

QUALITY TIME AND PHYSICAL TOUCH,
WITH A FEW YUMMY TREATS IN BETWEEN.

BOXERS ARE LOYAL:

THEY'LL BE RIGHT BY YOUR SIDE.

THEY'LL WATCH YOU AND FOLLOW YOU.
THERE'S NO PLACE YOU CAN HIDE!

BOXERS LOVE HUMANS, BUT ONE THING REMAINS:

PERSONAL SPACE IS NOT IN THEIR DOMAIN.

THEY MUST THINK THEY'RE LIGHT AS A FEATHER,
OR SMALL AS A BUG.

ESPECIALLY WHEN THEY GIVE YOU
A PROLONGED BODY HUG.

BOXERS HAVE SPIRIT, AND SPUNKY PERSONALITIES TOO.

THEY HAVE A PARTICULAR WAY OF SAYING "I LOVE YOU."

BOXERS CAN BE STUBBORN,
AND SOMETIMES TOUGH TO SWAY.

AVOIDANT, IMMOBILE, AND FICKLE
ARE THINGS THEY PORTRAY.

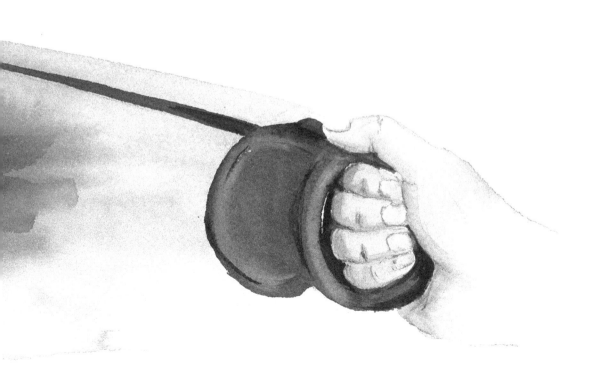

BOXERS HAVE TALENTS:
THESE COME WITH THE BREED.

THESE GIFTS INVOLVE MAKING
SPECIFIC DEMANDS OF WHAT THEY NEED.

THERE ARE SPECIAL THINGS THAT MAKE
BOXERS ENDEARING AND SWEET,

FROM THEIR BEAR SOUND EFFECTS
TO THEIR REINDEER PRANCING FEET!

BOXERS HAVE MOODS
THAT CAN CHANGE EVERY DAY:

THEY ALSO HAVE MODES
THAT ARE TO SLEEP AND TO PLAY.

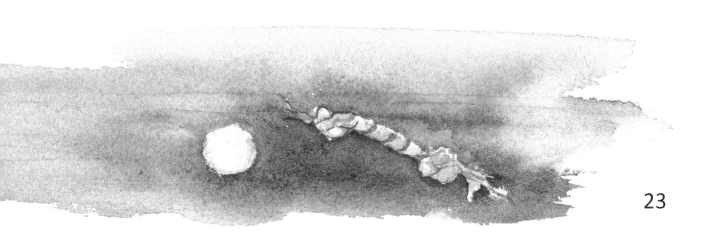

BOXERS BRING JOY TO WHOMEVER THEY MEET.

DON'T BE FOOLED: THEY ARE PROTECTIVE BUT SWEET.

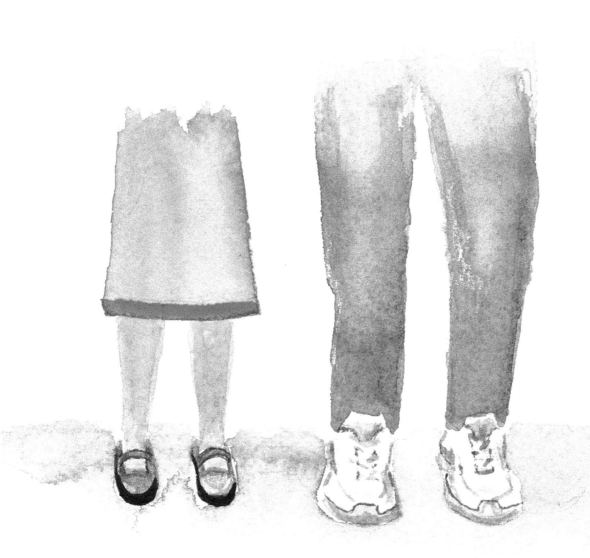

THEY KNOW WHAT TO DO
TO MAKE US FEEL LOVED,

THEIR SNUGGLES AND SNORTS
SECURE US LIKE A GLOVE.

BOXERS HAVE PECULIAR WAYS OF STEALING OUR HEARTS.

EVEN WHEN THEY SURPRISE US WITH STINKY, SMELLY FARTS!

BUT THERE'S ONE BOXER THAT'S SPECIAL TO KNOW,
FROM A NUB FOR A TAIL TO A CUTE, WET BLACK NOSE.

FROM TWO SILKY LITTLE EARS TO SIXTEEN FURRY TOES.
MEET BUBS WITH THE NUBS-LOOK, THERE HE GOES!

YOU SEE, "BUBS WITH THE NUBS" IS A NAME THAT WE SAY.

HIS REAL NAME IS TIMBER, BUT HE ANSWERS EITHER WAY.

BUBS WITH THE NUBS
HAS SOME NOTEWORTHY QUIRKS.

LIKE HOW HE EATS WATERMELON
RIGHT OFF A FORK!

AT NIGHTTIME, HE MIGHT LIKE
ANOTHER TREAT OR TWO.

PEANUT BUTTER IS SOMETHING
BUBS MIGHT ASK OF YOU.

HE'S CERTAIN TO BE WARM
UNDER THE BLANKETS AT NIGHT,

WRAPPED LIKE A BURRITO
SO COZY AND TIGHT.

BUBS WITH THE NUBS LOVES PEOPLE; IT'S TRUE.
WHEN HE SEES YOU, HE'LL HOP AROUND LIKE A KANGAROO!

CRAZY OR CALM, HE IS LOVED JUST THE SAME.
BUBS WITH THE NUBS WILL FOREVER BE HIS NAME.

ABOUT TIMBER, "BUBS WITH THE NUBS"

Timber was from West Virginia, where he was surrendered to a rescue dog organization called Boxer Transfer Network. Timber was adopted by Bethany and Micah Marshall in October of 2013 and went over the rainbow in December of 2022. Timber loved being with humans, and physical touch was his top love language. Timber was sweet, smart, and a creature of habit. He enjoyed peanut butter before bedtime every night. Timber's favorite treats to eat were watermelon, bananas, cantaloupe, sweet potatoes, cooked carrots, and vanilla ice cream.

TIMBER'S FRIENDS:

Boxer Transfer Network:

Thank you for rescuing Boxers just like Timber, and for all that you do to help our four-legged friends find their FUR-ever homes.

Hollidaysburg Animal Clinic:

We couldn't ask for a better team of veterinarians to help take care of Timber. Thank you for your love, professionalism, and kindness!

ABOUT THE AUTHOR: BETHANY MARSHALL

Bethany Marshall is the family life pastor at Trans4mation Church in Altoona, Pennsylvania. She is also the founder and director of Daughters Conference, a conference birthed out of her heart for daughters from all generations. Bethany currently resides in Altoona, Pennsylvania, with her husband, Micah, where they both serve in ministry. Bethany is the author of two other children's books: Pickles and Prayer and Pineapples and Praise. Bethany enjoys drinking dark roast coffee, shopping for good deals, and has loved pickles since she was a little girl.

ABOUT THE ILLUSTRATOR: SARAH VOGEL

As a mother of two boys and an entrepreneur, artist Sarah Vogel keeps more than busy in her hometown of Altoona, Pennsylvania. Sarah illustrated multiple children's books and even authored one herself. Her medium of choice is watercolor. Sarah enjoys mentoring employees at her combined coffee shop and roastery/pottery studio, painting fun foods in her at-home studio, crafting handmade jewelry, and helping anyone she meets to unleash their creativity and pursue their dreams.

Other Books by Bethany Marshall

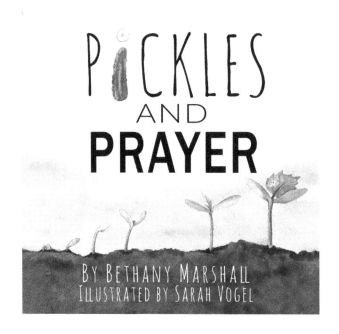

What could be more important than your child learning and discovering the power of prayer? *Pickles and Prayer* has lively illustrations that draw the attention of young readers. The colorful pages and poetic text will help your child understand that prayer is simple, but it is also powerful.

Pickles and Prayer also includes a homemade pickle recipe for the whole family to enjoy!

Also available in Spanish!

PINEAPPLES AND PRAISE

By Bethany Marshall
Illustrated by Sarah Vogel

We are all called to praise the Lord! *Pineapples and Praise* offers beautiful, colorful illustrations to awaken the wonder in a child's heart about God's design. From His Word to His handiwork, we can begin to understand God's great love for His children and the praise that He deserves.

Pineapples and Praise encourages readers to live with their eyes wide open, cultivating a heart of gratitude toward the One who made it all!

CPSIA information can be obtained
at www.ICGtesting.com
Printed in the USA
BVHW010437160223
658457BV00002B/3